Let's Explore

Air

by Henry Pluckrose

SEA-TO-SEA

Mankato Collingwood London

Author's note

This book is one of a series which has been designed to encourage young readers to think about the everyday concepts that form part of their world. The text and photographs complement each other, and both elements combine to provide starting points for discussion. Although each book is complete in itself, each title links closely with others in the set, so presenting an ideal platform for learning.

I have consciously avoided "writing down" to my readers. Young children like to know the "real" words for things, and are better able to express themselves when they can use correct terms with confidence.

Young children learn from the experiences they share with adults around them. The child offers his or her ideas, which are then developed and extended through the adult. The books in this series are a means for the child and adult to share informal talk, photographs, and text, and the ideas which accompany them.

One particular element merits comment. Information books are also reading books. Like a successful storybook, an effective information book will be turned to again and again. As children develop, their appreciation of the significance of fact develops too. The young child who asks "What is air?" may subsequently and more provocatively ask, "Where does it come from?" Thoughts take time to generate. Hopefully books like those in this series provide the momentum for this.

Henry Pluckrose

Contents

Wherever you are,
whether you're awake or asleep,
you are surrounded by air.
You can't see the air,
but it is all around you.

Air is a mixture of different gases.
It surrounds the Earth,
like an invisible blanket.

All living things need air.
When you breathe you can feel
the air going into your lungs.
Your lungs take oxygen from the air.
Without oxygen you would die.

Moving air is called wind.
We can't touch air,
but when it is windy
we can feel the air
moving around us.

We can't see the wind,
but as it blows we can see
the direction in which it is moving.

When the wind blows
it's fun to fly a kite.
The moving air holds
the kite up in the sky
as it twists and turns.

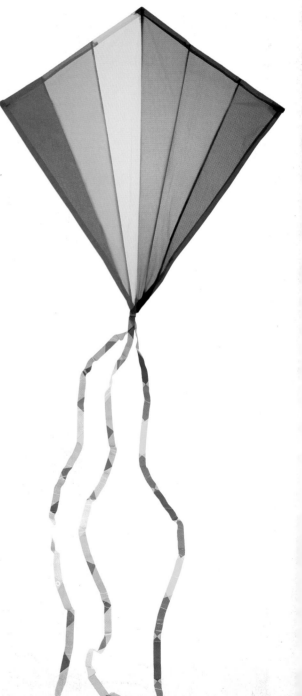

Hurricanes and tornadoes
are fast-moving winds.
They are so strong they destroy
everything in their path.

Wind can be used
to make machines work.
On a wind farm like this one,
the wind moves the propellers
and they produce electricity.

Air is used in lots of ways.
Armbands are filled with air
to keep you afloat in water.
The air in a padded jacket
helps keep you warm.
Do you know why bicycle tires
have air in them?

This hovercraft
floats on air.
Its engine blows out air
and makes a cushion
on which it can float
across land and water.

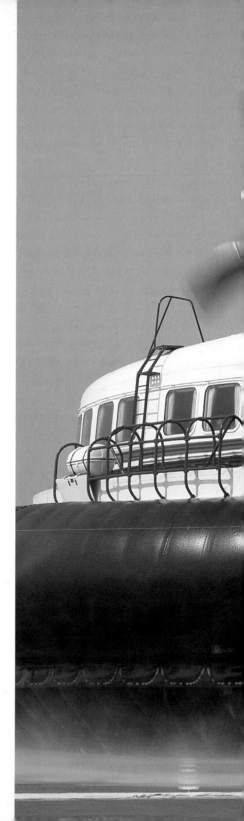

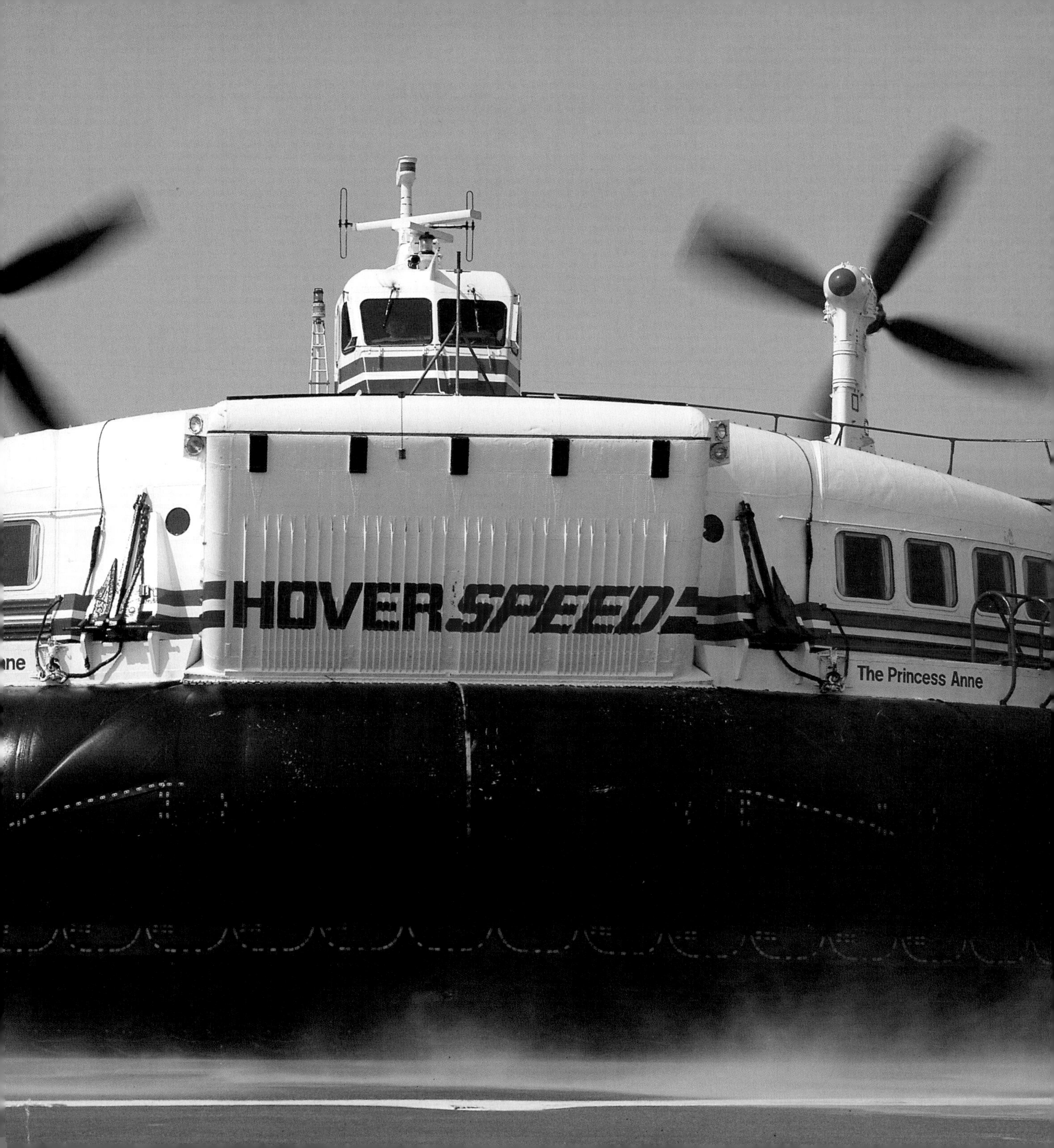

HOVERSPEED
The Princess Anne

When air is hot, it rises.
The air in this balloon
is heated by a special burner.
As the hot air rises, the balloon flies.

Birds fly through the sky.
Air moving above
and below their wings
helps hold them up.

Some cars, trains, and planes are shaped so they move smoothly through the air. Why do you think this is called a "bullet train"?

To stay healthy we need
to breathe clean air.
It is important that the air we breathe
is not polluted by cars and trucks,
or by smoke from factories.

Index

This edition first published in 2007 by
Sea-to-Sea Publications
1980 Lookout Drive
North Mankato
Minnesota 56003

Copyright © Sea-to-Sea Publications 2007

Printed in China

All rights reserved

Library of Congress Cataloging-in-Publication Data

Pluckrose, Henry Arthur
  Air / by Henry Pluckrose
    p. cm. -- (Let's explore, the elements set)
  Includes index.
  ISBN-13: 978-1-59771-033-6
    1. Air--Juvenile literature. 2. Atmosphere--
Juvenile literature. 3. Wind power--Juvenile
literature. I. Title.

QC161.2.P574 2006
551.5--dc22
                              2005058524

9 8 7 6 5 4 3 2

Published by arrangement with the Watts
Publishing Group Ltd, London

Series editor: Louise John
Series designer: Jason Anscomb

Picture Credits:
The Stock Market - cover photograph, p.9
(T & D McCarthy); Tony Stone Images
p.6 (Darryl Torckler), p.10 (Eddie Soloway); Images Colour
Library pp.19, 32 and title page, p.28; James Davis Travel
Photography p.12; Still Pictures p.31 (Thomas Raupach), p.27
(Thomas D Mangelsen); Robert Harding p.15 (Jon Gardey),
p.20 (Schuster / Dr. Müller), p.23 (David Hughes), p.24
(Schuster);Image Bank p.17 (A. T. Willett); Impact p.4
(Francesca Yorke); Steve Shott p.14.